Sheep

Julie Murray

Abdo
FARM ANIMALS
Kids

abdopublishing.com

Published by Abdo Kids, a division of ABDO, PO Box 398166, Minneapolis, Minnesota 55439.
Copyright © 2016 by Abdo Consulting Group, Inc. International copyrights reserved in all countries.
No part of this book may be reproduced in any form without written permission from the publisher.

Printed in the United States of America, North Mankato, Minnesota.

052015

092015

THIS BOOK CONTAINS
RECYCLED MATERIALS

Photo Credits: iStock, Shutterstock

Production Contributors: Teddy Borth, Jennie Forsberg, Grace Hansen

Design Contributors: Candice Keimig, Dorothy Toth

Library of Congress Control Number: 2014960326

Cataloging-in-Publication Data

Murray, Julie.

 Sheep / Julie Murray.

   p. cm. -- (Farm animals)

ISBN 978-1-62970-943-7

Includes index.

1. Sheep--Juvenile literature.   I. Title.

636.3--dc23

                      2014960326

Table of Contents

Sheep

Sheep live on farms.

Most sheep are white or brown. Some are black. Others have spots or **markings**.

Baby sheep are called lambs.

Boys are rams. Girls are ewes.

Sheep say, "baa."

Sheep eat grass and hay.

They also eat **grain**.

Sheep have thick hair called 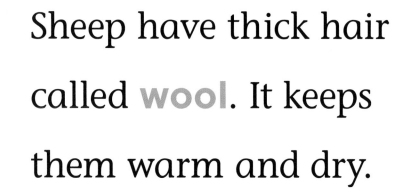wool. It keeps them warm and dry.

Sheep's **wool** is used to make clothes. Jack wears a wool sweater.

17

Hats can be made from wool.

Zoe stays warm!

Have you seen sheep on a farm?

A Sheep's Life

eat

get a haircut

drink water

hang out with the herd

Glossary

grain
the seeds of plants that are used for food.

marking
a mark or repeated mark on an animal's fur or skin.

wool
the soft curly hair that grows on sheep. It is used to make cloth and yarn.

Index

abdokids.com

Use this code to log on to abdokids.com and access crafts, games, videos, and more!

Abdo Kids Code:
FSK9437